STECK-VAUGHN

TOP LINE Math

Geometry

Harcourt Achieve

Rigby • Saxon • Steck-Vaughn

www.HarcourtAchieve.com
1.800.531.5015

Acknowledgments

Editorial Director	Ellen Northcutt
Supervising Editor	Pamela Sears
Senior Editor	Kathy Immel
Associate Design Director	Joyce Spicer
Design Team	Jim Cauthron
	Joan Cunningham
Photo Researcher	Stephanie Arsenault
Cover Art	©Janet Parke
Photography Credits	p. 6 ©Dennis MacDonald/PhotoEdit
	p. 18 Courtesy Sam Dudgeon/HRW photo
	p. 30 ©Adam Woolfitt/CORBIS
	p. 46 ©Tom Wagner/CORBIS/SABA
	p. 58 ©Kindra Clineff/Index Stock Imagery

ISBN 1-4190-0373-9

Contents

To the Student 2

Setting Goals 3

Pretest 4

UNIT 1
Basics of Geometry   6

Overview Lessons 1–4
Points, Lines, and Angles 7
   Lesson 1 Points and Lines 8
   Lesson 2 Parallel and Perpendicular Lines . . . 10
   Lesson 3 Angles 12
   Lesson 4 Pair of Angles 14
   Test-Taking Strategy: Draw a Diagram 16
UNIT 1 | Review   17

UNIT 2
Geometric Figures   18

Overview Lessons 5–8
Properties of Shapes 19
   Lesson 5 Properties of Triangles. 20
   Lesson 6 Properties of Quadrilaterals 22
   Lesson 7 Properties of a Circle 24
   Lesson 8 Circumference of a Circle 26
   Test-Taking Strategy: Make an Organized List . 28
UNIT 2 | Review   29

UNIT 3
Geometry and Measurement   30

Overview Lesson 9–14
Using Formulas 31
   Lesson 9 Area of a Rectangle 32
   Lesson 10 Area of a Triangle. 34
   Lesson 11 Area of a Circle 36
   Lesson 12 Similar and Congruent Figures . . . 38
   Lesson 13 Symmetry. 40
   Lesson 14 The Pythagorean Theorem. 42
   Test-Taking Strategy: Use a Formula 44
UNIT 3 | Review   45

UNIT 4
Coordinate Geometry   46

Overview Lessons 15–18
Geometry and the Coordinate Plane 47
   Lesson 15 Translations 48
   Lesson 16 Reflections 50
   Lesson 17 Rotations 52
   Lesson 18 Dilations 54
   Test-Taking Strategy: Find a Pattern 56
UNIT 4 | Review   57

UNIT 5
Three-Dimensional Figures   58

Overview Lessons 19–23
Properties of Solids 59
   Lesson 19 Properties of Solids. 60
   Lesson 20 Surface Area Using Nets: Cylinder . . 62
   Lesson 21 Surface Area Using Nets:
       Rectangular Prisms 64
   Lesson 22 Volume of a Cylinder. 66
   Lesson 23 Volume of a Cone 68
   Test-Taking Strategy: Write an Equation 70
UNIT 5 | Review   71

Post Test 72

Glossary 74

Math Toolkit 77

Review Your Progress . . . . Inside Back Cover

To the Student

Building a solid foundation in math is your key to success in school and in the future. Working with the *Top Line Math* books will help you to develop the basic math skills that you use every day. As you build on math skills that you already know and learn new math skills, you will see how much math connects to real life.

When you begin reading the Overview in this *Top Line Math* book, read the **You Know** and **You Will Learn** sections. As you focus on new math skills, consider how they connect to what you already know.

Pretest and Post Test

Take the Pretest at the beginning of this book. Your results on the Pretest will show you which math skills you already know and which ones you need to develop.

When you have finished working in this book, take the Post Test. Your results on the Post Test will show you how much you have learned.

Practice

Practice pages allow you to practice the skills you have learned in the lesson. You will solve both computation problems and word problems.

Unit Reviews

Unit Reviews let you see how well you have learned the skills and concepts presented in each unit.

Test–Taking Strategy

Every test-taking strategy shows you various tools you can use when taking tests.

Glossary

Each lesson has **key words** that are important to know. Turn to the glossary at the end of the book to learn the meaning of new words. Use the definitions and examples to strengthen your understanding of math terms.

Setting Goals

A goal is something you aim for, something you want to achieve. It is important to set goals throughout your life so you can plan realistic ways to get what you want.

Successful people in all fields set goals. Think about your own goals.

- Where do you see yourself after high school?
- What do you want to be doing 10 years from now?
- What steps do you need to take to get to your goals?

Goal setting is a step-by-step process. To start this process, you need to think about what you want and how you will get it. Setting a long-term goal is a way to plan for the future. A short-term goal is one of the steps you take to achieve your long-term goal.

What is your long-term goal for using this book about geometry? You may want to improve your test scores or you may want to become better at math so you can become a home builder.

Write your long-term goal for learning math.

_____

_____

Think about how you already use geometry. Then, set some short-term goals for what you would like to learn in this book. These short-term goals will help you to reach your long-term goal.

I use geometry in my everyday life to

☐ paint, design, or make crafts.

☐ figure out the shortest distance to a destination.

☐ sketch out where furniture will fit in a room.

☐ _____

My short-term goals for using this book are

_____

_____

Pretest

Take this Pretest before you begin this book. Do not worry if you cannot easily answer all the questions. The Pretest will help you determine which skills you are already strong in and which skills you need to practice.

Identify the lines A and B as parallel, perpendicular, or intersecting but not perpendicular.

1. _____

2. _____

Identify each angle as acute, right, obtuse or straight.

3. _____

4. _____

Find the supplement for each angle.

5. 45° _____

6. 72° _____

Use this diagram for problems 7 and 8.

7. Identify all drawn radii of circle O.

8. *MO* is 4 cm. Find the circumference of circle O.

Find the area of each figure.

9. A circle with a diameter of 4 yd.

10.

Use the similar figures in this diagram to answer questions 11 and 12.

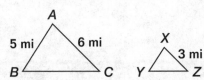

11. How long is side *XY*?

12. What angle corresponds to ∠*Z*.

Find the coordinates of each point after the given transformation.

13. Where is the image of point $(2, 4)$ after a $(-3, 4)$ slide?

14. Where is the image of point $(5, 3)$ after a flip over the *x*-axis?

15. Where is the image of point $(2, -1)$ after a 90° clockwise rotation around $(0, 0)$?

16. Where is the image of point $(-1, -4)$ after a dilation with its center at $(0, 0)$ and a scale factor of 2?

Find the volume of each figure.

17.

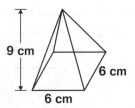

18.

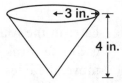

Find the surface area.

19.

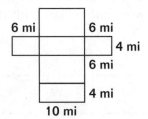

20.

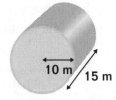

Real-Life Matters

You are practicing a new routine for the marching band state championship. The band director asks you to line up and march in parallel rows, turn 45° to face right, and then make a 90° right turn. You need to understand points, lines, angles, and other basics of geometry to march correctly. To win, the band's routine will need to be perfect.

Real-Life Application

The first move is to march in 3 parallel lines. What exactly does "to march in parallel lines" mean?

_____

_____

Later in the routine, the person at the head of each line turns 45° right. After finishing this move, the lines turn 90° right. What direction are you now heading after you make these 2 turns?

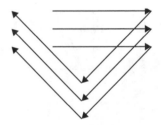

_____

Next, the people in your line and another line have to march through each other in perpendicular lines. What is the angle your line makes with the other line as the 2 lines cross?

_____

_____

Points, lines, and planes are the building blocks of geometry.

Overview • Lessons 1–4

Points, Lines, and Angles

Geometric shapes are all around us. Windows and doors are rectangles. Many roofs are shaped like triangles. Cups and plates are circular. Even street signs are based on geometric shapes.

Suppose you want to design a logo for your band. What do you need to know about points, lines, and angles to make a better logo? In this unit, you will learn to identify and use the geometry basics of points, lines, and angles.

YOU KNOW

- How to add and subtract

- The names of several shapes

YOU WILL LEARN

- The definition of a point, a line, a plane, and an angle

- How to recognize parallel and perpendicular lines

- About the relationships of different angles

Remember the BASICS

Solve.

1. $180 - 37 = 143$

2. $90 + 56 =$

3. $24 = 10k$

4. $9b = 36$

Solve.

5. What is the area of a rectangle with a length of 11 cm and a width of 7 cm?

6. What is the area of a square with sides measuring 16 cm each?

7. What is the next figure in the pattern?

  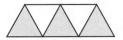 

Points and Lines

Points, lines, and angles are the building blocks of geometry. The tiles that make up this floor are repeated copies of the same simple shapes.

Art, nature, and the shapes that surround us every day are made up of points, lines, and angles.

A **point** is an exact location. It has no size, shape, or direction.

A **line segment** has 2 endpoints. An endpoint names where a line starts and stops. Use endpoints to name a line segment.

A **line** is a straight path that extends without end in opposite directions. Use 2 points on a line to name a line.

A **plane** is like the flat surface of this page. But like a line, a plane goes on forever. Lines and points can be on a plane.

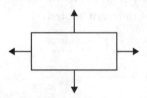

A **ray** has one endpoint and then goes on without stopping in one direction only. Use the endpoint as the first letter when naming a ray.

Example

Look at the drawing. How many of the geometric parts can you identify?

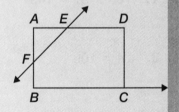

STEP 1 How many points are there?
Remember, a point marks a position but has no size, shape, or direction. There are 6 points.

STEP 2 How many segments are there?
A segment is a part of a line. It has a point where it starts and stops. There are 9 segments in the figure.

STEP 3 What else is in the drawing?
6 rays and 1 line.

ON YOUR OWN

Look at this figure. How many geometric parts can you identify?

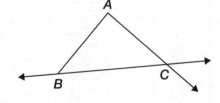

Practice

Building Skills

Find the number of parts.

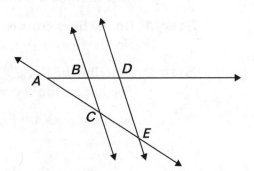

1. How many line segments are in this figure?

   There are 4 line segments. $\overline{AC}$ $\overline{BC}$ $\overline{CD}$ $\overline{BD}$

2. How many points does the figure have?

Use this figure to answer questions 3 and 4.

3. How many line segments make up the sides of this figure?

4. How many points make up the corners of this figure?

Use this figure to answer questions 5 and 6.

5. How many rays are in the figure?

6. How many lines are in the figure?

Use this figure to answer questions 7 and 8.

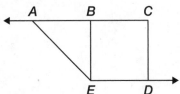

7. How many points are at the corners of this figure?

8. How many line segments make up the figure?

Problem Solving

Use the figure on the right to answer numbers 9–12.

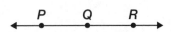

9. Name 3 different line segments.

   Possible answers: $\overline{PQ}$, $\overline{PR}$, $\overline{QR}$

10. Name 4 different rays.

12. Give another name for the ray RQ.

11. Give 6 names for this line.

13. Name at least 4 parts of the geometric figure on the right.

Parallel and Perpendicular Lines

Sometimes lines are drawn in special ways. **Parallel** lines are in the same plane. But parallel lines never meet and have no common points. Train tracks are examples of parallel lines. **Perpendicular** lines **intersect,** or cross, to form square corners.

Think of two pencils as straight lines. If the pencils can lie on the same piece of paper or plane, the same distance apart, and are *not* intersecting, then they are **parallel.** If the pencils intersect and form 4 corners, then they are **perpendicular.**

You can identify lines as parallel (∥), perpendicular(⊥), or intersecting (lines that cross each other, but are not perpendicular).

Example

Are the lines shown parallel, perpendicular, or intersecting (and not perpendicular)?

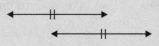

Step 1 Do the lines cross each other?
No, the lines do not cross, so they are not perpendicular or intersecting.

Step 2 Describe the lines.
The lines are in the same plane and are an equal distance apart.

So, these lines are parallel.

ON YOUR OWN

Are the lines shown parallel, perpendicular, or intersecting (and not perpendicular)?

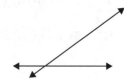

Practice

Building Skills

Identify the pairs of lines as parallel, perpendicular, or intersecting but not perpendicular. Use this figure for questions 1–10.

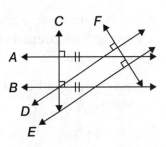

1. *A* is _____ to *D*.

   A is intersecting but not perpendicular to *D*.

2. *A* is _____ to *C*.

3. *D* is _____ to *E*.

4. *C* is _____ to *D*.

5. *B* is _____ to *A*.

6. *D* is _____ to *B*.

7. *C* is _____ to *F*.

8. *D* is _____ to *F*.

9. *A* is _____ to *F*.

10. *E* is _____ to *F*.

Problem Solving

Describe how the lines are related.

11. The yard lines on a football field

    The yard lines on a football field are drawn equal distances apart and do not cross. They are parallel.

12. The edges of a poster that form a corner

13. Draw a line through the center of a pyramid that is perpendicular to the ground. Trace a line along one edge of the base of the pyramid.

14. The white line on the edge of a road and a post that holds a stop sign

15. The rungs of a ladder

16. The strings of a guitar

When two lines come together at the same point, they form an **angle** (∠). The point where the lines come together is called the **vertex** of the angle. Three letters (points) name an angle. The middle letter is the vertex. The angle shown is ∠ABC or ∠B.

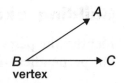

Angles come in different sizes and are measured in degrees (°). A **protractor** measures angles.

Angles also have special names based on their size or measure. The table below includes the names of the different types of angles.

Angle Name	Measure	Hints and Facts
acute	Between 0° and 90°	An acute angle is smaller than a right angle.
right	90°	There's a small square in the corner of a right angle. Squares have right angles.
obtuse	Between 90° and 180°	An obtuse angle is bigger than a right angle.
straight	180°	Lines form straight angles.

Example

What type of angle is shown?

STEP 1 Is the angle a right angle or a straight angle?
It is neither a right angle nor a straight angle.

STEP 2 Compare it to a straight angle.
It is smaller than a straight angle, so it is either obtuse or acute.

STEP 3 Compare it to a right angle.
The angle is smaller than a right angle.

So, it is acute.

ON YOUR OWN

What type of angle is shown?

Practice

Building Skills

Name each type of angle.

1.

> The angle is bigger or wider than a right angle. So this is an obtuse angle.

2.

3.

4.

5.

6.
A

7.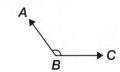
A
B → C

8. P ———— R
S

9. M
N
P

Problem Solving

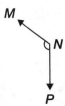

132°
48°
48°
132°

Solve.

Use this figure for questions 10–12.

10. What are the measures of the acute angles?

> An acute angle measures less than 90°. The angles measuring 48° are acute angles.

11. What are the measures of the obtuse angles?

12. If you add a 48° angle to a 132° angle, what type of angle have you made?

13. The pointed end of a pizza slice measures 30°. How many of these slices would make up the entire pizza? [Hint: a circle is 360°.]

14. A skateboard ramp measures 45° up from the ground. What is the measure of the angle between the ramp and the ground in front of it?

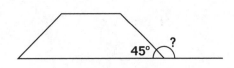

45° ?

Sometimes one angle relates in a special way to another angle. For example, some pairs of angles are always equal to each other. Some pairs add to 180° or 90°.

If you have a pair of parallel lines and a line that intersects them, the lines form 8 angles: ∠A, ∠B, ∠C, ∠D, ∠E, ∠F, ∠G, ∠H. The pairs of angles created by the intersecting line have special relationships with each other. When angles are formed by a line intersecting two parallel lines, the **corresponding angles** are in the same position along a different parallel (||) line. Corresponding angles are equal in measure.

Corresponding Angles

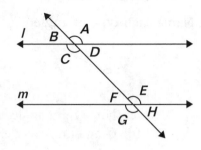

$$\angle A = \angle E = \angle C = \angle G$$
$$\angle B = \angle F = \angle D = \angle H$$

Vertical Angles
When two lines intersect, the opposite angles are **congruent,** equal in size.

Complementary Angles
Two angles whose sum equals 90° are **complementary.**

Supplementary Angles
Two angles whose sum equals 180° are **supplementary.**

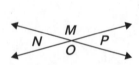

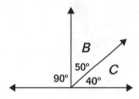

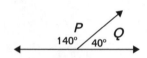

∠M = ∠O   ∠N = ∠P

∠B + ∠C = 90°

∠P + ∠Q = 180°

Example

If ∠B in the diagram at the top of the page is 56°, what is the measure of ∠F?

STEP 1 What is the position of the pair of angles?
∠B and ∠F are in the same position (top right) in the intersections of each of the parallel lines, *l* and *m*.

STEP 2 Classify the angles.
∠B and ∠F are corresponding angles.

STEP 3 What is the relationship between the angles?
Corresponding angles are equal.

So, ∠F is 56°.

ON YOUR OWN

Find the measure of an angle that is supplementary to a 126° angle.
[Hint: Supplementary angles add to 180°.]

Practice

Building Skills

Find the measure of each angle.

Use this figure for questions 1–10.

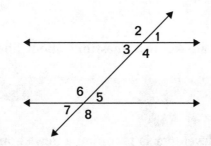

1. If ∠1 is 42°, what is the measure of ∠7?

   Because the lines are parallel, ∠7 is equal to its corresponding ∠3, and ∠3 is vertical to ∠1. So ∠7 = ∠3 = ∠1 = 42°.

2. If ∠5 is 50°, what is the measure of ∠8?

3. If ∠2 is 150°, what is the measure of ∠4?

4. If ∠6 is 124°, what is the measure of ∠5?

5. If ∠8 is 140°, what is the measure of ∠4?

6. If ∠2 is 112°, what is the measure of ∠6?

7. If ∠2 is 112°, what is the measure of ∠8?

8. If ∠1 is 25°, what is the measure of ∠5?

9. If ∠1 is 35°, what is the measure of ∠8?

10. If ∠4 is 146°, what is the measure of ∠6?

Problem Solving

Solve.

11. You try to parallel park and the angle that your tire forms with the curb is 27°. What obtuse angle does the other side of the curb form with your tire?

    The angle you want is supplementary to the 27° angle.
    180 − 27 = 153
    The angle measures 153°.

12. While riding your motorcycle, you brake hard to miss hitting a dog. Your tire leaves a skid mark as you come to a stop. The skid mark forms four angles when it crosses the painted line on the side of the road. One angle formed is 62°. What other angles are formed?

Draw a Diagram

Drawing a diagram can help you answer test questions about lines and angles.

Example

A real estate developer is planning a new shopping area that includes many stores. It will be located on five parallel streets that form perpendicular intersections with four other parallel streets (going in the opposite direction). One store will be built on every small lot surrounded by four streets. How many stores will be built in the new shopping area?

STEP 1 Draw a diagram of the streets.

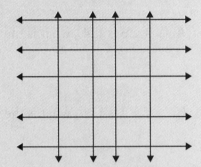

STEP 2 Count the number of small squares.
There are 12 small squares.

Twelve stores will be built in the shopping area.

TRY IT OUT

The intersection of Hamilton Road and North Street forms a right angle. Maple Street starts at the intersection and runs between Hamilton Road and North Street. What type of angle do Maple Street and North Street form?

Circle the correct answer.

A. acute   B. right   C. obtuse   D. straight

Option A is correct. An acute angle is smaller than a right angle.

How many line segments, rays, or lines make up each of these shapes?

1.

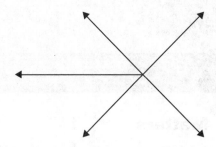

2.

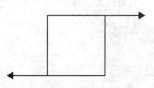

_____

_____

Are the lines parallel, perpendicular, or neither?

3.

4.

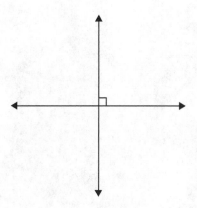

_____

_____

Name each type of angle as acute, right, obtuse, or straight.

5.

6.

_____

_____

Find the measure of each angle.

7. ∠B _____

8. ∠D _____

9. ∠F _____

10. ∠H _____

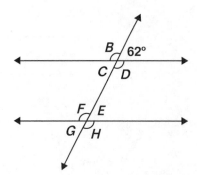

Geometric Figures

Real-Life Matters

You are playing a game where you have to draw picture clues of objects for your team to guess. You pick a card that says *chair*. You would have to draw *chair* so that your team could guess it. Your card could say any object like *bridge, nuts and bolts, house,* or *the Pentagon*. To draw any of these words, you would need to know basic geometric figures.

Real-Life Application

Your teammate picks *train*. She wants to pass, but if she does your team loses a point and a turn. You are allowed to give your teammate clues, but then you cannot guess. You whisper some clues to her. What are they?

_____

_____

Your teammate chooses *honeycomb* and is stumped. You smile and whisper the name of a basic geometric figure. Your teammate nods and begins to draw several of the figures side by side. What geometric figure does your teammate draw?

_____

_____

Overview • Lessons 5–8

Properties of Shapes

In these lessons, you will learn how to put points, lines, and angles together to make figures. You will also learn about circles, which do not have any straight sides or corner points.

Bridges, highway supports, and many other structures are built by connecting triangles. Triangles are used because their shape makes them sturdy and strong. Observatories are circular to allow for open space.

YOU KNOW

- Properties of points, lines, planes, and angles

- Properties of parallel and perpendicular lines

YOU WILL LEARN

- Properties of triangles and quadrilaterals

- Properties of circles

Remember the BASICS

Find the missing angle.

1. $62° + 37° + \underline{\hspace{2cm}} = 180°$

2. $90° + 48° + \underline{\hspace{2cm}} = 180°$

3. $152° + 28° + 152° + \underline{\hspace{2cm}} = 360°$

4. $90° + 62° + 143° + \underline{\hspace{2cm}} = 360°$

Properties of Triangles

A **triangle** is a **polygon** with 3 sides, 3 angles, and 3 vertices. The sum of the angles in a triangle equals 180°.

Triangles have 3-letter names. You name a triangle by using the letters of the vertices.

Triangles can be classified by the length of their sides or the size of their angles.

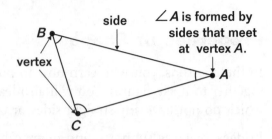

side

∠*A* is formed by sides that meet at vertex *A*.

vertex

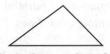

A scalene triangle is a triangle whose sides all have different lengths.

An isosceles triangle is a triangle that has two sides of the same length.

An equilateral triangle is a triangle whose sides are all the same length.

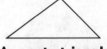

An acute triangle is a triangle whose angles all are acute.

An right triangle is a triangle with one right angle.

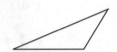

An obtuse triangle is a triangle with one obtuse angle.

Example

Find the missing angle in the triangle.

STEP 1 Add the two given angles.
angle *QPR* (90°) + angle *PQR* (40°)
90° + 40° = 130°

STEP 2 Subtract this answer from 180°.
180° − 130° = 50°

Angle *PRQ*, the third angle, is 50°.

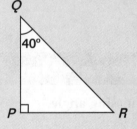

ON YOUR OWN

Find the third angle in this triangle.

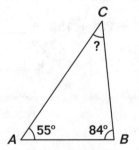

Practice

Building Skills

Classify each triangle as an acute, obtuse, or right triangle. Then, find the measure of the missing angle in each.

1.

Unknown angle: $64 + 52 + n = 180$
$n = 64$
Acute triangle

2.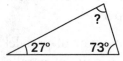

3.

Problem Solving

Use triangle properties to solve these problems.

4. You are building shapes from colored rods with your nephew. You have a 2-in. rod and 2 5-in. rods. If you make a triangle, what type of triangle will you make?

Two of the sides are the same length, 5-in. each. A triangle having two sides of the same length is an isosceles triangle.

5. You go for a run on three roads that form a triangle. You know that the first and second roads are 0.8 mi and 1.3 mi long. The third road is 2 miles long? Which type of triangle does this arrangement form?.

6. A line supporting a volleyball net breaks. You reattach a rope to the pole at a 55° angle and place the stake in the ground. The pole now stands perpendicular to the ground. What angle does the rope make with the ground?

7. Because each triangle has angles that add to 180°, how many degrees do the angles in this hexagon add up to? (Hint: Count the number of triangles in the hexagon.) Explain.

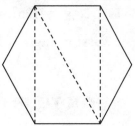

9. Draw an acute scalene triangle.

8. A chair's back, arm, and seat forms a triangle. The angle formed between the seat and arm measures 35°. The angle formed by the seat and back measures 77°. What is the measure of the angle formed by the back and arm?

Properties of Quadrilaterals

All **quadrilaterals** have four sides, four angles, and four vertices. No matter what the shape of the quadrilateral, the four angles always add to 360°.

Rectangles and squares are common quadrilaterals.

The relationships between sides and angles give each special type of quadrilateral its specific name and properties.

A **trapezoid** is a quadrilateral with only one pair of parallel sides. A **parallelogram** is a quadrilateral with two pairs of parallel sides. Parallelograms also have their opposite sides equal and opposite angles equal.

A **rectangle** has four right angles, and its opposite sides are equal.

A **rhombus** has four equal sides that are parallel.

A **square** has four equal sides and four right angles.

Kites have two adjoining sides equal.

Understanding these properties can be helpful when you need to find certain answers about these shapes.

On tests, you may be asked to find missing angles. With quadrilaterals, you just subtract the sum of the three other angles from 360°.

Trapezoid

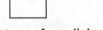
Parallelogram

Rectangle, a type of parallelogram

Rhombus, a type of parallelogram

Square, a type of rectangle

Kite

Example

Find the measure of the missing angle.

STEP 1 Add the known angles together.
90° + 115° + 30° = 235°

STEP 2 Subtract the answer in Step 1 from 360°.
360° − 235° = 125°.

The missing angle is 125°.

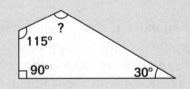

ON YOUR OWN

Find the measure of the missing angle.

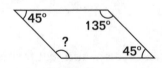

Practice

Building Skills

Use this figure for questions 1–4.

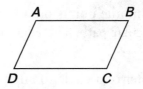

1. In parallelogram *ABCD*, if ∠*A* = 155°, what is the measure of ∠*B*?

   Because of the properties of parallelograms ∠*A* = ∠*C*, so ∠*A* + ∠*C* = 155° + 155° = 310°. All the angles in a parallelogram add up to 360°, So this leaves 360° − 310° = 50° for ∠*B* + ∠*D*.

   ∠*B* = ∠*D*, so ∠*B* + ∠*D* = 2 × ∠*B*

   2 × ∠*B* = 50°, so ∠*B* = 25°

2. In parallelogram *ABCD*, if ∠*D* = 30°, what is the measure of ∠*A*?

3. In parallelogram *ABCD*, if $\overline{AB}$ is 10 cm long, and $\overline{BC}$ is 5 cm long, how long is $\overline{CD}$?

4. In parallelogram *ABCD*, if $\overline{AB}$ is 6-in. long, and $\overline{DA}$ is 2-in. long, how long is $\overline{BC}$?

Problem Solving

Solve.

5. Your neighborhood swimming pool is a rectangle that is 9 ft wide and 15 ft long. How far is it around the whole pool?

   Because opposite sides of a rectangle are equal, the perimeter (distance around the edges) is 9 ft + 15 ft + 9 ft + 15 ft = 48 ft

6. A flag has a parallelogram on it that contains a 45° angle. What are the measures of the other 3 angles?

7. Every baseball diamond has 4 equal distances between bases and 90° angles connecting the bases. What type of shape connects the 3 bases and home plate?

8. Two angles of a quadrilateral are 25° and 35°. The third angle is twice the measure of the fourth angle. What are the measures of the third and fourth angles?

Properties of a Circle

A circle is a closed set of infinite points on a line. Picture a sprinkler watering in a circular path. The edge of the circle is the circumference.

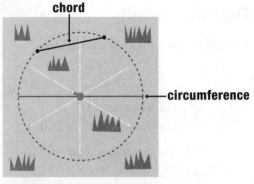

The distance from the center of a circle to any point on the edge is called the **radius.** A line segment whose endpoints lie on the circle is called a **chord.** A chord that goes through the center of the circle is called a **diameter.** Notice that the diameter is always twice as long as the radius. Every circle = 360°.

radius + radius = diameter

Example

If $\overline{AB}$ is 20 in., what is the measurement of $\overline{AO}$?

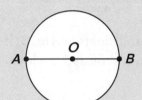

STEP 1 Define the lines.
$\overline{AO}$ is the radius. $\overline{AB}$ is the diameter.

STEP 2 Set up the problem.
Since a radius is half the diameter, divide 20 by 2.
20 ÷ 2 = 10

$\overline{AO}$ is 10 in.

ON YOUR OWN

If $\overline{AB}$ is 6.5 in. what is the measure of $\overline{AC}$?

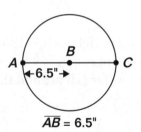

$\overline{AB}$ = 6.5"

Practice

Building Skills

Solve.

Use these figures for questions 1–8.

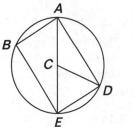
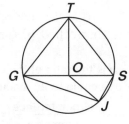

1. Name one radius in circle *C*.

$\overline{CA}, \overline{CD},$ or $\overline{CE}$ are all radii.

2. Name two radii of circle *O*.

3. Name a line segment in circle *C* that is not a chord.

4. Name the sides of inscribed ∠*B*.

5. How many chords are shown in circle *O*?

6. What are the two shortest chords in circle *C*?

7. $\overline{SG}$ is a diameter. What is the sum of the central angles ∠*SOJ* and ∠*GOJ*?

8. $\overline{GS}$ is a diameter of circle *O*, and ∠*TOS* = 86°. What is the measure of ∠*TOG*?

Problem Solving

Solve.

Use the figures above for questions 9 and 10.

9. In a triangle, angles that are opposite from equal sides are equal. Use this fact to help find the measure of ∠*OJG* if ∠*GOJ* is 150°.

All radii in a circle are equal, so *OG* = *OJ*, ∠*OJG* = ∠*OGJ*. The angles on a triangle add to 180°, so 180° − 150° = 30°.

10. If ∠*TOS* = 86°, find the measure of ∠*OTS*.

11. You are buying wheel covers for your car. The diameter of your wheels is 28 in. Wheel covers are sold by radius size. What is the correct radius size for your wheels?

12. You have 3 points on a circle and you connect them. What is the sum of the 3 inscribed angles you formed? [Hint: Think about the sum of the angles in a triangle]

13. On the exercise bikes in the gym, the speedometer is a circle. Every 10° of the central angle is 0.5 miles per hour (mph). What is the measure of the central angle between 0 mph and 5.5 mph?

14. You divide a meat pie into 5 equal pieces. What is the central angle that each piece forms?

LESSON 8   Circumference of a Circle

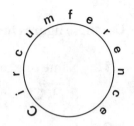

Once you can find the radius and diameter of a circle, you can also find the distance around the circle.

This distance around the edge of a circle is called the **circumference.**

The circumference of a circle is always equal to the length of the diameter times a number called **pi**. The symbol for pi is π and is equal to about 3.14.

> **pi** is the ratio of the circumference of a circle to its diameter.
>
> $$\pi = \frac{\text{circumference}}{\text{diameter}} = 3.14$$

To find a circumference of a circle, multiply the radius by 2 times π.

> Circumference of a circle:
> $C = 2\pi \times r$ or
> $C = 2\pi r$

You can also use $\frac{22}{7}$ as the value for *pi*.

Example

What is the circumference of a circle with a radius of 8 m?

STEP 1 Use the formula for circumference.
$C = 2\pi r$

STEP 2 Put the numbers in the formula and solve.
You know that the diameter is 8 m.
$\pi \approx 3.14$
$C = 2 \times 3.14 \times 8 = 50.24$ m

$C = 50.24$ m

ON YOUR OWN

What is the circumference of a circle with a radius of 4 cm?

Practice

Building Skills

Find each distance. Use 3.14 for π.

1. What is the circumference of a circle with a diameter of 4 ft?

> If the diameter is 4 ft, then the radius is 2 ft
> $2(3.14) \times 2 = 12.56$

2. What is the circumference of a circle with a radius of 5 mm?

3. What is the circumference of a circle with a diameter of 19 yd?

4. What is the circumference of a circle with a radius of 2 mi?

5. What is the circumference of a circle with a diameter of 3 cm?

6. What is the circumference of a circle with radius of 6 in.?

7. What is the circumference of a circle with radius of 4.5 m?

8. What is the diameter of a circle with circumference of 18 ft?

Problem Solving

Solve using the formula for circumference. Use 3.14 for π.

9. A bicycle wheel has a diameter of 36 in. How far does it go each time the wheel turns all the way around?

> The radius is one half the diameter.
> $C = 2\pi \times r$
> $C = 2 \times 3.14 \times 18 = 113.04$ in.

10. A CD has a radius of about 5 cm. How far is it around the edge of the disc?

11. A plastic flying disk has a diameter of 1 ft. What is the circumference?

12. A trainer has a horse on a 16-ft length of rope. The horse walks in a circle around the trainer. How far has the horse walked if it walks around the trainer once?

TEST–TAKING STRATEGY

Make an Organized List

You can make an organized list to help you answer test questions about geometric shapes.

Example

Andrea bought this painting at an art show. What shape appears most often in the painting?

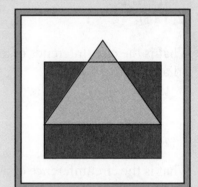

STEP 1 Make an organized list to show all of the possible answers (geometric shapes).
- The painting has a square.
- The painting has 2 rectangles (including the square).
- The painting has 4 triangles.

STEP 1 Look for additions to the list (less obvious answers).
If lines rather than color define a shape, what other shapes are in the painting?
- There is another rectangle.
- There are 2 quadrilaterals.
- There is 1 hexagon.

STEP 3 Find the answer to the question from the data in the list.

The shape that appears most often in the painting is a triangle.

TRY IT OUT

Shapes are made out of line segments. Use the same painting. How many line segments are there in Andrea's painting? [Hint: It will help to label all points.]

Circle the correct answer.

A. 7   B. 11   C. 10   D. 18

Option D is correct. There are 9 points and 18 ways to make line segments.

Find the measure of each missing angle.

1.

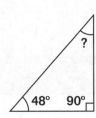

48° 90°

2.

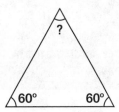

60° 60°

3.

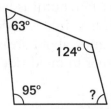

63°
124°
95° ?

4.

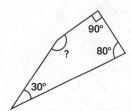

90°
? 80°
30°

Use this diagram to answer questions 5–6.

5. ∠A in the parallelogram ABCD measures 42°. Find the measure of ∠B.

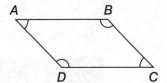

A   B

D   C

6. AB is 3 cm long, and BC is $\frac{1}{2}$ as long as AB. What is the perimeter of parallelogram ABCD?

Use this diagram to answer questions 7–8.

7. Identify the chord(s) in circle M.

8. $\overline{OP}$ = 7 cm. Find the circumference of circle M.

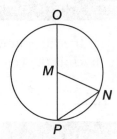

O

M

N

P

Draw and define each triangle.

9. equilateral triangle

10. isosceles triangle

11. obtuse triangle

12. right triangle

Geometry and Measurement

Real-Life Matters

Amusement parks are great fun, but it is hard work to build one. As each new ride is added, the park planners need to think about areas, distances, and shapes in order to build rides and put them in the best spots.

Real-Life Application

Imagine that you are making the plan for some new amusement park buildings and rides. You will need to answer questions about area, dimensions, and cost to convince the park owner that your plan is the best.

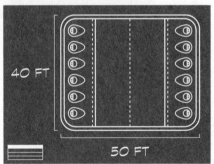

How would you find the area of the bumper car ride?

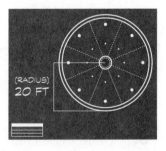

The merry-go-round takes up about 1300 square feet. If the work to prepare the site comes to $15,000, approximately how much is the cost per square foot?

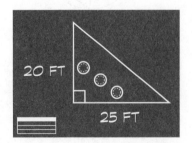

The park planners set up the ring toss in a triangular booth. What are two ways to figure out the long side of the booth, one with a ruler and one without a ruler?

There are formulas in geometry that help you find lengths, areas, volumes, and angle measures. By learning the formulas and what each variable stands for, you will be able to solve many problems.

Overview • Lessons 9–14

Using Formulas

A formula is a way of expressing a relationship between two or more quantities. To make a frame, you have to know how much wood to buy and that depends on how big you want the frame to be. You would measure the length and the width to find the dimensions of the frame. Using the formula $P = 2l + 2w$ will tell you how much wood to buy.

To fill a swimming pool, you need to know how deep, wide, and long the pool is. An easy way to find out is to use $V = l \times w \times h$

Architects, designers, and artists use formulas everyday to do their work.

YOU KNOW

- Properties of certain geometric figures

- How to work with ratios

- How to work with squares and square roots

YOU WILL LEARN

- To find areas

- To use similarity

- The Pythagorean theorem

Remember the BASICS

Answer the questions. You will later use the same type of skills to help find areas and other measurements of geometric figures.

1. A parallelogram has a perimeter of 20 m and one side of 6 m. How long is the other side?

   $20 = 2(6) + (2)(L)$
   $20 = 12 + 2L$
   $20 - 12 = 2L$
   $8 = 2L$
   $4 = L$

2. $\dfrac{2}{3} = \dfrac{?}{18}$

3. $8^2 = ?$

4. What is the square root of 144?

   $\sqrt{144} = ?$

5. What is the radius of a circle with a circumference of 56.52 ft?

Rectangles are all around you. Most rooms, walls, doors, and windows are rectangles. To find out how much paint or carpeting to buy, you would have to know the area of the door or floor.

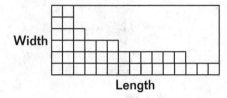

Width

Length

Area is the measure of the space inside a flat figure. Imagine a tile floor. The total number of squares that it will take to cover the rectangle above is exactly equal to the number of rows times the number of columns, which is the same as length times width.

> **Area of a rectangle = Length × Width**
> **or $A = l \times w$**

Another thing to remember is that squares have equal lengths and widths.

Example

Find the area of this rectangle.

3 cm
6 cm

STEP 1 Write the area formula for a rectangle.
$A = l \times w$

STEP 2 Put the numbers you know into the formula.
$A = 3 \text{ cm} \times 6 \text{ cm} = 18 \text{ sq cm or } 18 \text{ cm}^2$

The area is 18 cm².

ON YOUR OWN

Find the area of this rectangle.

3.5 mi
10 mi

Practice

Building Skills

Solve.

1. Find the area of the rectangle.

2 ft
5 ft

$A = l \times w$
$A = 5 \times 2 = 10 \text{ ft}^2$

2. Find the area of the rectangle.

1 mm
3.5 mm

3. Find the area of the rectangle.

32 km
100 km

4. Find the measure of the width.

$A = 100 \text{ sq cm}$?
20 cm

5. Find the measure of the length.

$A = 72 \text{ sq yd}$
2 yd
?

6. Find the measure of the length.

$A = 15 \text{ sq mi}$ 3 mi
?

Problem Solving

Solve.

7. A dance floor has an area of 450 sq ft. The length of the dance floor is 25 sq ft. What is the width?

$A = l \times w$
$450 = 25 \times w$
$w = 18 \text{ ft}$

8. What is the area of a $20 bill that measures 2.5 in. by 6 in.?

9. How many sq ft of lumber do you need to build a 6 ft by 4 ft rectangular platform for a tree house?

10. The area of a tent floor is 38.5 sq ft. The length is 7 ft. What is the width?

11. How much will it cost you to buy a 3.5 ft by 12 ft rectangular banner for your school pep rallies if it costs $0.50 per sq foot?

12. You are doing the layout for the school newspaper and each page is 150 sq in. If you have already included three 1.5 in. by 6 in. cartoons on one page, can you fit 135 sq in. of text on the same page or do you need to cut some text? Explain.

Now that you can find areas of rectangles, you can use a similar method to find the area of a triangle.

> **Area** $= \dfrac{1}{2} \times$ **base** $\times$ **height or** $A = \dfrac{1}{2}bh$

The base can be any side of the triangle. The height is a line drawn from the top of the triangle and perpendicular to the base or an extension of the base.

In a right triangle, the height is one side of the triangle.

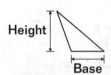 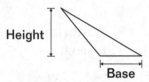

Example

Find the area of the triangle below.

STEP 1 Write the formula to find the area of a triangle.

$$A = \dfrac{1}{2}bh$$

STEP 2 Put the numbers you know into the formula.

$$A = \dfrac{1}{2} \times 3 \text{ cm} \times 4 \text{ cm} = 6 \text{ sq cm}$$

STEP 3 Solve.

The area of the triangle is 6 sq cm.

ON YOUR OWN

Find the area of this triangle.

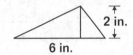

Practice

Building Skills

Solve.

1. Find the area of the triangle.

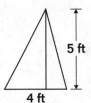

$$A = \frac{1}{2}bh$$
$$A = \frac{1}{2} \times 4 \text{ ft} \times 5 \text{ ft} = 10 \text{ sq ft}$$

2. Find the area of the triangle.

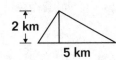

3. Find the area of the triangle.

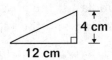

4. Find the height.

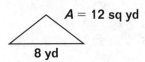

A = 12 sq yd

5. Find the height.

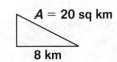

A = 20 sq km

6. Find the base.

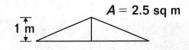

A = 2.5 sq m

Problem Solving

Solve.

7. How many square feet is a triangular sail if the base is 8 ft and the sail is 9 ft high?

$$A = \frac{1}{2}bh$$
$$A = \frac{1}{2}(8)(9)$$
$$A = 36 \text{ sq ft}$$

8. You start to fold an airplane out of a piece of paper and have a triangle that has a base of 8.5 in. and a height of 11 in. What is the area of this triangle?

9. How much fabric do you need to make a triangular flag that is 1 yd wide and has a base of 1.5 yd?

10. You are painting a house, and one outside wall is a rectangle with a triangle on top of it. What is the area of this wall?

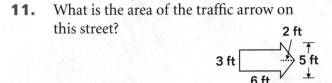

11. What is the area of the traffic arrow on this street?

12. A triangular shaped hang glider has an area of 60 sq ft. The wings are 12 ft from tip to tip. What is the distance from the front to the back of the glider?

LESSON 11   Area of a Circle

You have already learned the formula for the distance around the edge of a circle, or the circumference.

Circumference = 2 × π × **r**, or **C = 2πr**

The formula for the area of a circle also uses the value for the radius and the value of pi (π).

Area of a circle = π × **radius**^{2} or **A = πr^2** ← exponent, $r^2 = r × r$

In the same way you did with rectangles and triangles, you can use this formula to find the area if you know the radius, or to find the radius if you know the area.

$C = 2πr$ and $A = πr^2$

Example

Find the area of the circle. For π use 3.14.

STEP 1 Write the formula for the area of a circle.
$A = πr^2$

STEP 2 Put the number you know into the formula and solve.
$A = 3.14 × (3 \text{ cm})^2 = 28.26 \text{ cm}^2$

The area of this circle is 28.26 cm^2.

ON YOUR OWN

Find the area of the circle.

Practice

Building Skills

Solve. Use 3.14 for π.

1. Find the radius of the circle.

Area = 12.56 ft^2

$A = \pi r^2$
$12.56 = 3.14 r^2$
$4 = r^2$
$2 = r$
The radius is 2 ft.

2. Find the area of the circle.

4 km

3. Find the area of the circle.

20 yd

4. Find the radius of the circle.

A = 113.04 cm^2

5. Find the radius of the circle.

A = 78.5 yd^2

6. Find the diameter of the circle.

A = 153.86 m^2

Problem Solving

Solve. Use 3.14 for π.

7. What is the area of a circular parachute that measures 14 ft across the center?

If the diameter is 14 ft, then the radius = 7 ft.
$A = \pi r^2 = 3.14\,(7)^2 = 153.86\ \text{ft}^2$

8. You see an old photo of your grandparents playing with a large circular hoop. If the diameter of the hoop is 4 ft, what is the area inside it?

9. Your class has been asked to paint a big smiley face on the pavement in front of the school stadium. You have enough paint to cover 200 sq ft. To the nearest foot, how big should the radius of the circle be? Use 3.14 for π.

10. Each ring of this archery target is 2 in. wide, and the bull's-eye is 4 in. across. What is the area of the entire target?

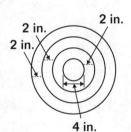

2 in.   2 in.

2 in.

4 in.

LESSON 12 Similar and Congruent Figures

With geometric figures, if two figures are the same, then you say they are **congruent. Congruent** figures have the same shape and same size. If you know that two figures are congruent, then you know that their measurements are the same.

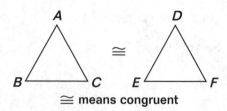

≅ means congruent

If two figures are **similar,** it means that the figures have the same shape and that the corresponding angles are equal.

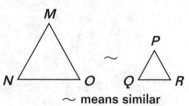

∼ means similar

Figures are similar if they have the same proportions. The rectangles are similar.

$$\frac{3}{5} = \frac{6}{10}$$

Example

Barbara had a 3-in.-by-5-in. photo enlarged to a 6-in.-by-10-in. photo. Is the enlargement similar to the original?

STEP 1 Find the ratio of the lengths.

$$\frac{5}{10}$$

STEP 2 Find the ratio of the widths.

$$\frac{3}{6}$$

STEP 3 Set up a proportion.

$$\frac{5}{10} \diagup\!\!\!\!\diagdown \frac{3}{6}$$
$$30 = 30$$

Yes, they are similar because they are proportional.

ON YOUR OWN

A regulation high school basketball court is 50 ft × 84 ft. A college court is also 50 ft wide but is 94 ft long. Is the college court similar to the high school court?

Practice

Building Skills

Find the length of each side.

Use this diagram for questions 1–3.
$MNOP \cong GHIJ$.

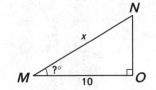

1. $\overline{MP}$

> *MP* corresponds to
> *GJ*, and because the
> figures are congruent
> the sides are equal.
> $\overline{MP}$ = 2 yd

2. $\overline{OP}$

3. $\overline{GH}$.

Use these triangles for problems 4–6.
$ABC \sim MNO$.

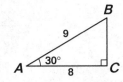

4. What is the measure of $\angle M$?

5. What is the length of side x?

6. What are the measures of $\angle B$ and $\angle N$?

Problem Solving

Solve using the rules of similarity and congruence.

7. You are enlarging a picture and want the two rectangles to be similar. The width went from 1 in. to 12 in. The height was $\frac{2}{3}$ in. How tall will the final picture be?

> To be similar, each pair of sides needs to be in the same ratio. Here the ratio is 1:12, so to find the height, multiply $\frac{2}{3}$ in. by 12 and get $\frac{24}{3}$ in., or 8 in.

8. On a certain day, every motorcycle that comes off an assembly line is congruent. If the first motorcycle's rear wheel has a diameter of 22 in., what is the diameter of the rear wheel on the 37th motorcycle?

9. You have a 3-ft-high and 5-ft-long flag. If a huge flag in a parade is similar and 15 ft high, how long is it?

10. Are the areas of congruent figures always the same? Explain.

LESSON 13 Symmetry

Some figures have **symmetry**. A figure has symmetry if it can be folded so that the two parts of the figure match. The line across the figure is a **line of symmetry**.

Some figures have no line of symmetry.

 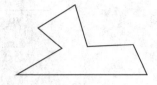 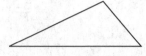

Some figures have only 1 line of symmetry.

 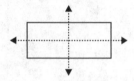

Some figures have more than 1 line of symmetry.

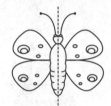 

Example

How many lines of symmetry are in the triangle?

STEP   Draw in a line to split a figure into congruent halves. Congruent means equal.

This triangle has 3 lines of symmetry.

ON YOUR OWN

How many lines of symmetry are there in a square?

Practice

Building Skills

Solve.

Use this figure to answer questions 1 and 2.

1. How many lines of symmetry does this regular pentagon have?

> A regular pentagon has a line of symmetry from each vertex (⊥) to the other side. So there are 5 lines of symmetry.

2. How many new angles are formed at the place where the lines of symmetry cross?

Use this figure to answer questions 3 and 4.

3. How many lines of symmetry does this figure have?

4. Where the lines of symmetry cross, are the angles equal?

Use this figure to answer questions 5 and 6.

5. How many lines of symmetry does this arrow have?

6. What does this arrow look like folded in half?

Use this figure to answer questions 7 and 8.

7. How many lines of symmetry does this smiley face have?

8. Does this smiley face look the same for all lines that can cut it in half? Explain.

Problem Solving

Solve using symmetry.

9. Does a yin/yang symbol have symmetry?

> Because of the color difference, there is no way you can draw a line of symmetry so that one side will be a mirror-image of the other side.

10. How many lines of symmetry does a soccer field have?

11. Which numerical digits have symmetry?

12. Which capital letters have symmetry? (Don't include cursive letters.)

13. Does a starfish have a line of symmetry? Explain.

14. All regular figures follow a pattern with lines of symmetry. Use this pattern to find the number of lines of symmetry on a regular 10-sided figure.

The Pythagorean Theorem

Patterns appear throughout geometry. One of the most famous is the relationship between the sides in a right triangle. The special formula, known as the **Pythagorean theorem,** helps you find distances between points on a coordinate plane, find missing triangle side lengths, or determine if a triangle has a right angle.

The formula for the Pythagorean theorem is: $a^2 + b^2 = c^2$

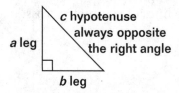

If three triangle side measurements work in the formula, then you know you have a right triangle.

Example

Find the length of the third side in this right triangle.

3 cm

4 cm

STEP 1 Write out the formula.
$$a^2 + b^2 = c^2$$

STEP 2 Put the numbers you know into the formula.
$$3^2 + 4^2 = c^2$$

STEP 3 Solve.
$$3^2 + 4^2 = 9 + 16 = 25 \qquad c^2 = 25$$
$$\sqrt{25} = 5 \qquad c = 5$$

The length of the third side is 5 cm.

ON YOUR OWN

A ladder is placed against the side of a building at 24 ft. The ladder is 25 ft tall. How far away from the building is the ladder?

Practice

Building Skills

Solve.

1. Do the sides of a triangle measuring 7 in., 24 in., and 25 in. make up a right triangle?

   $a^2 + b^2 = c^2$
   $7^2 = 49, \ 24^2 = 576$ and
   $25^2 = 625$, and $49 + 576 = 625$,
   so the triangle is a right triangle.

2. Do the sides 12 cm, 15 cm, and 20 cm make up a right triangle?

3. Find the missing side.

   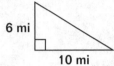

4. Find the missing side.

   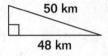

5. Find the missing side.

   50 km
   48 km

Problem Solving

Solve using the Pythagorean theorem.

6. How far is it from corner to corner of a 50-yd-by-100-yd rectangular field? Hint: Draw a picture.

   $50^2 = 2,500, 100^2 = 10,000,$
   $2,500 + 10,000 = 12,500$
   $\sqrt{12,500} \text{ yd} = 50\sqrt{5} \text{ yd} \approx 110 \text{ yd}$

7. Televisions are measured by the diagonal distance across the screen. Your television screen has a 40-in. diagonal and a height of 25 in. How wide is the screen?

8. A baseball diamond is a square with 90 feet on each side. How far is it between home plate and second base?

9. You have a 20-ft cord on your electric guitar from your speaker in the corner of your garage. If the garage is 17 ft wide and 12 ft long, can you reach the opposite corner? Explain.

10. You are setting up a tent for an outdoor party. You want to make sure that the poles are at right angles to the ground. Each pole is 2 m high and the tie ropes are 2.5 m long. How far (in meters) from the poles should you put the stakes to make right triangles?

11. Your science class is trying to design high-flying kites. You use 40 ft of string to fly the kite. Your friend stands under the kite and is 30 ft away from you. How high is your kite flying? Hint: Draw a picture.

Use a Formula

Knowing a formula can help you find an answer easily.

Example

The screen on an LCD TV is the shape of a rectangle. The area of the screen is 240 sq in. The length is 20 in. What is the width of the screen?

STEP 1 Write the formula.
$A = l \times w$

STEP 2 Put the numbers you know into the formula.
$264 = 20 \times ?$

STEP 3 Solve.
$240 = 20x$
$\dfrac{240}{20} = x$
$12 = x$

STEP 4 Check your answer.
$A = l \times w$
$A = 20 \times 12$
$A = 240$

The screen is 12 in. wide.

TRY IT OUT

A school parking lot is the shape of a square. It has an area of 1,225 sq yd. What is the length of each side of the parking lot?

Circle the correct answer.

A. 30 yd   **B.** 32 yd   **C.** 35 yd   **D.** 38 yd

Option C is correct. $A = s^2 = 1{,}225$; $s = \sqrt{1{,}225} = 35$.

Find the area of each figure.

1. 4 m [rectangle] 10.5 m

2. [triangle] 2 in. 3 in.

3. [circle] 10 ft

Use the triangles below to answer questions 4–7. *ABC is congruent to DEF.*

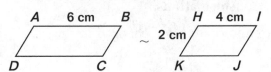

6 km *A* *B* *C* ≅ *D* 41° *E* 8 km *F*

4. How long is $\overline{DE}$?

5. What angle corresponds to ∠*F*?

6. How long is $\overline{BC}$?

7. What is the measure of ∠*D*?

Use these figures to answer questions 8–11.

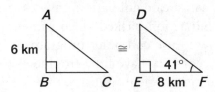

A 6 cm *B* ~ 2 cm *H* 4 cm *I* *D* *C* *K* *J*

8. How long is $\overline{AD}$?

9. What is the ratio of the $\overline{BC}$ to $\overline{IJ}$?

10. Write a proportion that shows these figures are similar.

11. Does ∠*A* equal ∠*D*? Explain.

How many lines of symmetry do each of these figures have?

12.

13. [parallelogram]

Solve.

14. $3^2 + ? = 5^2$

15. Find the missing side.

12 mm 16 mm

Coordinate Geometry

Real-Life Matters

Computer programs can create animation, movies with special effects, and action-packed video games. People who know how to use computer programs based on coordinate geometry have little trouble finding work in the entertainment industry. Coordinate geometry enables a computer program to take images and change their shape or move them around.

Real-Life Application

Suppose that your job is assisting a special effects designer. Your task is to double-check the following changes, or **transformations.**

Where would point **A** end up after it is changed in the following ways?

Reflected, as in a mirror, around the line $y = 3$

_____

Moving 90° clockwise around another point (3, 2)

_____

A shift in position, 5 units up and 12 units to the right

_____

If square **ABCD** has two corner points at (0, 3), and (0, 7), how would you name the other two corner points?

_____

Translations include *sliding, turning, flipping, stretching,* and *shrinking.* You can combine different types of translations to make things appear in all sorts of ways.

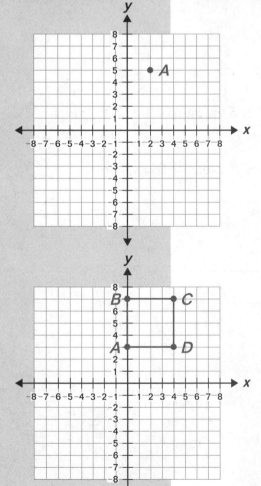

Overview • Lessons 15–18

Geometry and the Coordinate Plane

By using points, segments, and arcs on a plane, you can create geometric shapes. When designing a quilt, a coordinate plane is sometimes used to help create the pattern for each shape created as part of the quilt. By using a coordinate plane, the person making the quilt can be sure to create a pattern that has specific dimensions.

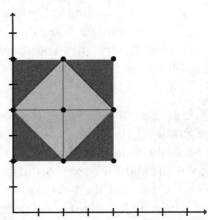

YOU KNOW

- Similar and congruent figures
- Symmetry

YOU WILL LEARN

- How to work with coordinates
- How to perform transformations

A **coordinate plane** is a lined grid used to find locations in relation to a center point, or origin. If someone asks, *What are your coordinates?* The question is really, *Where are you?* Points are given coordinate names that help you to find their location.

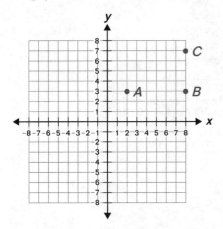

Sometimes geometric shapes are changed, or transformed, with slides, flips, turns, and stretches—also called *translations, reflections, rotations,* and *dilations.*

Remember the BASICS

Find the number of lines of symmetry on each figure.

1.

2.

3.

4.

LESSON 15 Translations

The coordinate plane is made up of two number lines that are perpendicular to one another. The horizontal line is the *x*-axis. The vertical line is called the *y*-axis. You can name a point on the coordinate plane by using a pair of numbers, an *x*-coordinate and a *y*-coordinate, (*x*, *y*). The point where the *x*-axis and *y*-axis cross is called the **origin,** (0, 0).

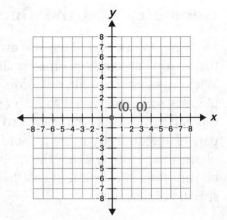

A **translation** is when you *slide* a figure to a new location on a coordinate plane. Every point in the figure slides in the same direction and the same distance. The **slide coordinates (*x*, *y*)** shows the direction and the distance of the slide. The *x*-coordinate, tells how far right or left to slide the figure, and the *y*-coordinate tells how far up or down it moves. The new figure is called an **image.**

Example

Translate the triangle below using the slide coordinates (3, −2).

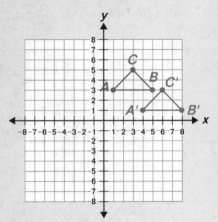

STEP 1 Add the slide coordinates to the points in the figure.
Add *x*-coordinates together and then *y*-coordinates to find the new points.
For example, if point *A* is (1, 3), then the new point, *A*′, is (1 +3, 3 + −2) = (4, 1).
The coordinates *A* (1, 3), *B* (5, 3), *C* (3, 5) become *A*′(4, 1), *B*′(8, 1), *C*′(6, 3).

STEP 2 Draw the *image* on the coordinate plane.

ON YOUR OWN

Translate the rectangle *MNOP* by sliding it (−2, 4).

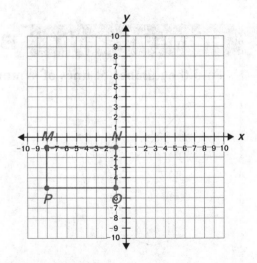

Practice

Building Skills

Solve each translation problem.

Use this diagram for problems 1–4.

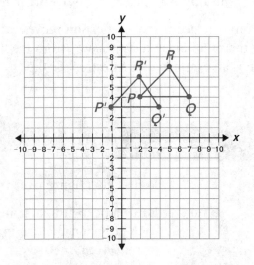

1. What are the points of the new image after a $(-3, -1)$ slide.

> After you slide each point, you get $P'(-1, 3)$, $Q'(4, 3)$, $R'(2, 6)$.

2. Draw the figure using the slide coordinates $(2, 0)$.

3. What are the points of the image after a $(2, 6)$ slide?

4. Draw the figure using the slide coordinates $(0, -3)$.

Problem Solving

Use translations to solve these problems.

5. A roller coaster car moves from the ground to the top of a hill 14 m left and 10 m up from the starting place. If the point it begins at is $(0, 0)$, what are the coordinates of the roller coaster's new point?

> The translation is $(0 + -14, 0 + 10)$ $= (-14, 10)$.

6. An ice skater slides 10 ft left and 5 ft forward. If the skater started 3 ft left and 8 ft in front of a gate, how far is he from the gate at after the slide? Let the gate be $(0, 0)$.

7. You are riding a canoe from the dock and go 50 ft north and 30 ft east, and then go 20 ft south and 15 ft east. How far from the dock are you after the two translations (moves)?

8. A map of the city shows 10 blocks across labeled 1–10H and 10 blocks going up and down labeled 1–10V. If you start at block $(2H, 5V)$ and walk 3 blocks east and 2 blocks south, where do you end up?

LESSON 16 Reflections

Look at yourself in the mirror. You may notice that your right and left sides are in opposite places in your mirror image.

In coordinate geometry, a **reflection** moves each point in a figure to a place that is an equal distance away from the line of reflection. A mirror image is an example of a reflection, or flip.

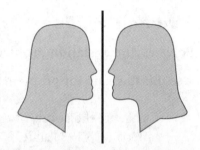

Example

Reflect this figure over the *y*-axis.

STEP 1 Draw a perpendicular line segment from each point on the original figure to the line of reflection, the *y*-axis.

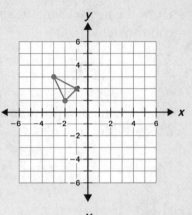

STEP 2 Draw the same line segments on the other side of the reflection line. Connect the points.

STEP 3 Plot the coordinates. Locate the points of the new image on the coordinate plane: (1, 2), (2, 1), (3, 3).

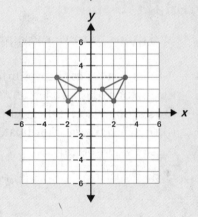

ON YOUR OWN

Reflect this figure over the *y*-axis.

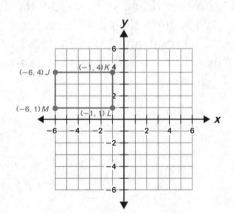

Practice

Building Skills

Solve each reflection problem.

Use this figure to answer questions 1–4.

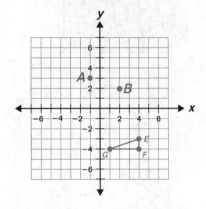

1. If you reflect the point A across the x-axis, where is its image?

   Point A reflects across the x-axis and becomes the point A'(−1, −3)

2. If you reflect the point B across the x-axis, where is its image?

3. If you reflect figure EFG across the y-axis, what are the coordinates of the image?

4. If you reflect figure EFG across the x-axis, what are the coordinates of the image?

Use this figure to answer questions 5 and 6.

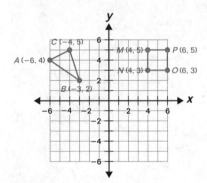

5. If you reflect the triangle ABC around the x-axis, where are the corners of the new image?

6. If you reflect the square MNOP around the y-axis, where are the corners of the new image?

Problem Solving

Solve using reflections.

7. You raise your left hand in a mirror. In the image, would you see your right or left hand?

   The image is a reflection of your left hand, but it looks like your right hand.

8. A camera flips the image over a line when it records it on film. When the film is developed, the image is flipped back over the same line. Explain why this double flip gives back the original view?

In geometry, a rotation is a figure that has been turned around a point. Clock hands are an example of figures being rotated.

To rotate a figure, you need to know three things:

- the **turn center,** also called the **point of rotation**
- the direction—clockwise or counterclockwise
- the angle of rotation

Example

Rotate triangle *ABC* 180° clockwise around the point of rotation (origin).

STEP 1 Put your pencil at the origin, (0, 0). Lay your pencil down on the page so that one end is on the origin and the rest of the pencil aligns with the triangle.

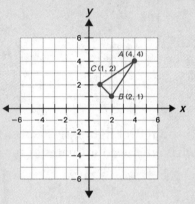

STEP 2 Turning the pencil clockwise, imagine the figure turns 180°. Use the tip of the pencil at the origin as a pivot point and twirl the pencil around.

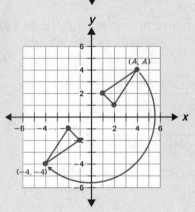

ON YOUR OWN

Rotate the figure 90° counterclockwise.

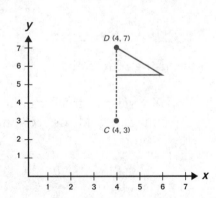

Practice

Building Skills

Solve each rotation problem.

**Use this diagram to answer questions 1–2.
Find the coordinates of each image.**

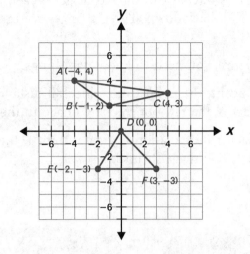

1. Rotate triangle *ABC* around point *C*
   90° clockwise.

2. Rotate triangle *DEF* around the origin
   180° counterclockwise.

3. Rotate the figure below 90° clockwise.

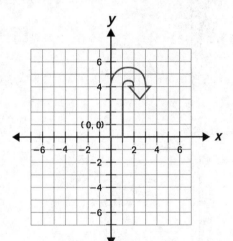

4. Rotate the letter *C* 180° clockwise.

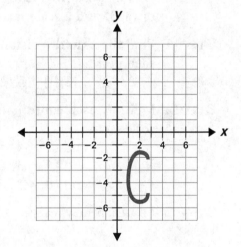

Problem Solving

Solve using rotations.

5. How much of a rotation is the movement
   of a clock hour hand from 2:00 to 4:00?

   12 hours make up 360°, 1 hour is 360°/
   12 = 30°. 2 hours = 2 × 30° = 60°

6. If a driver needs to make a u-turn, what
   should be the angle of rotation—90°, 180°,
   or 360°? Explain.

7. The volume knob on a stereo has 10
   volume marks evenly spaced around 270°.
   From the 0 mark, where would the 11th
   mark go in this rotation?

8. There are about 12 hours from sunrise to
   sunset. If the rotation of the sun is about
   180° in that time, how many degrees does
   the sun appear to rotate in one hour?

LESSON 18 Dilations

What happens when you blow up a balloon with the words *Happy Birthday* on it? The balloon stretches and the words get bigger. When you let the air out, the words shrink back down. These changes are examples of **dilations,** or stretches.

To dilate a figure, you need to know two things:

- the **center point,** the point from which all distances are measured
- the **scale factor,** the ratio of the new image to the original figure

If the scale factor in a dilation is greater than 1, the image stretches, and if it is smaller than 1, the image shrinks.

Example

Dilate figure *ABC* using the center of (0, 0) and a scale factor of 3.

STEP 1 Find the *x*- and *y*-distance(s) to each point.
A (0, 0) B (2, 4) C (2, 0)

STEP 2 Multiply each coordinate by the scale factor.
A (0 × 3) and (0 × 3) = A' (0, 0)
B (2 × 3) and (4 × 3) = B' (6, 12)
C (2 × 3) and (0 × 3) = C' (6, 0)

STEP 3 Plot each new image.

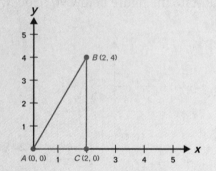

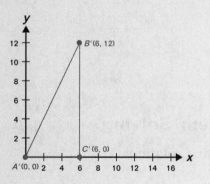

ON YOUR OWN

Dilate figure *ABC* using a scale factor of 2.

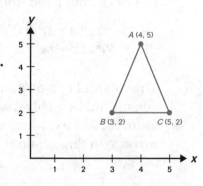

Practice

Building Skills

Solve each dilation problem. Use this diagram to answer questions 1–4.

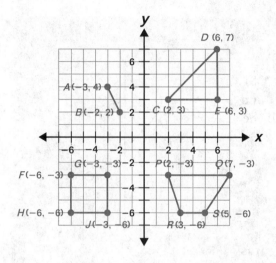

1. Where is the image of figure *CDE* after a dilation with center at $(0, 0)$ and a scale factor of 2?

$C' = (2 \times 2)$ and $(3 \times 2) = (4, 6)$
$D' = (6 \times 2)$ and $(7 \times 2) = (12, 14)$
$E' = (6 \times 2)$ and $(3 \times 2) = (12, 6)$

2. Where is the image of figure *FGHJ* after a dilation with the center at $(0, 0)$ and a scale factor of 0.5?

3. Where is the image of figure *PQRS* after a dilation with the center *P* and a scale factor of 0.25?

4. Where is the image of segment $\overline{AB}$ after a dilation with center at $(0, 0)$ and a scale factor of $\frac{1}{2}$?

Use this diagram to answer questions 5 and 6.

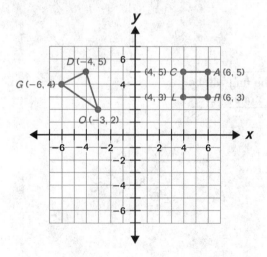

5. Where is the image of triangle *DOG* after a dilation with the center at $(0, 0)$ and a scale factor of 2?

6. Where is the image of rectangle *CARL* after a dilation with the center at $(0, 0)$ and a scale factor of 0.5?

Problem Solving

Use dilations to solve these problems.

7. A word on an empty balloon is 2 in. long. After you blow up the balloon, the word scales up by a scale factor of 8. How long is the word on the inflated balloon?

2 in. $\times$ 8 = 16 in.

8. Your TV has a picture-in-picture option. The smaller picture is 5 in. wide. The larger picture is a dilation centered in the middle of the small picture with a scale factor of 6. How wide is the large-screen picture?

Find a Pattern

Finding a pattern can help you answer test questions about transformations.

The flag below was moved from position A to position B, from position B to position C, and from position C to position D. Where will the flag be moved next?

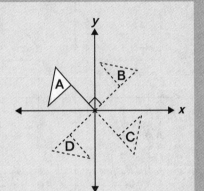

STEP 1 Find a pattern that describes how the flag was moved from one position to the next.
Pattern: In each movement to a new position, the flag was rotated 90° clockwise.

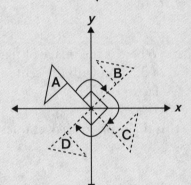

STEP 2 Continue the pattern to show the next position.
Rotate the flag another 90° clockwise.

The flag will be moved here

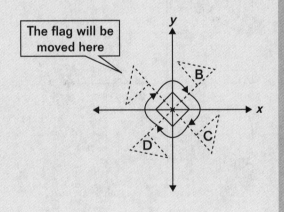

If the flag above is moved two more times following the same pattern, where will it be? Draw the new position on a coordinate grid.

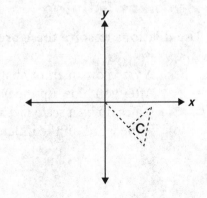

Find the coordinates of each point after the transformation. Use this diagram for questions 1 and 2

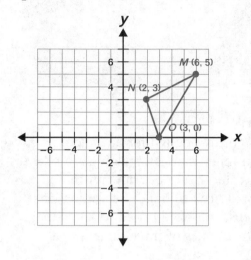

1. Where is the image of figure *MNO* after a $(-3, -1)$ slide?

_____

2. Where is the image of figure *MNO* after a reflection over the *x*-axis?

_____

Find the coordinates of each figure after the given transformation. Use this diagram to answer questions 3–6.

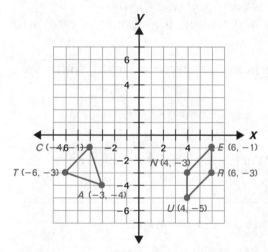

3. Where is the image of triangle *CAT* after a $(2, -3)$ slide?

_____

4. Where is the image of parallelogram *RUNE* after a flip over the line $x = 3$?

_____

5. Where is the image of triangle *CAT* after a 180° rotation around the origin?

_____

6. Where is the image of parallelogram *RUNE* after a dilation centered at point *R* with a scale factor of 2?

_____

Solve.

7. You are sitting at a baseball game and after a few innings you see a seat closer to the field. What type of transformation best describes your move?

_____

8. A race car driver makes 100 laps around a circular track. How many degrees does the car rotate around the center point of the track?

_____

Real-Life Matters

How would you create a design for an indoor skating rink? You might start by building a model to scale. Then, you could figure out how much material you would need to build the skating rink. To build the model, you would need to know the surface areas and volumes of three-dimensional (3-D) shapes.

Real-Life Application

If you use cardboard to make the model building, how would you determine the amount of cardboard you needed?

Three-dimensional objects have length, width, and height.

Use what you know about the surface area of squares.

Each wall measures 12 in. by 8 in. What is the area of the four walls?

Use what you know about the surface area of rectangles.

How would you find the surface or area of the roof?

Use what you know about the surface area of triangles.

At each end of the building there is a triangle shape supporting the roof. The triangle is 4 in. high and the base is 12 in. What is the area of each triangle?

You can build on what you know about areas of different figures to find the surface areas and volumes of many 3-dimensional objects.

Overview • Lessons 19–23

Properties of Solids

The box that holds your favorite cereal is manufactured as a flat piece of cardboard. It is only later in the process that it is folded and glued together to form the box. The flat piece of cardboard has length and width. It is a like a two-dimensional object. The box, on the other hand, is a three-dimensional object; a shape with length, width and height.

WHOLE WHEAT SQUARES

WHOLE WHEAT SQUARES

In this unit, you will work with shapes that have height, as well as length and width. These **three-dimensional (3-D) shapes** are called **solids.**

 or

In this unit, you will learn about two types of solids that have either round bases or polygon bases. The **base** is the bottom of a 3-dimensional shape.

These solids will have either two bases, like a prism, or one base, like a cone or a pyramid.

One base

or

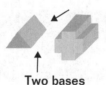

Two bases

YOU KNOW

- How to find areas of polygons
- How to find areas of circles

YOU WILL LEARN

- How to find surface areas of prisms and cylinders
- How to find volumes of prisms and cylinders
- How to find volumes of pyramids and cones

Remember the BASICS

Find the area of each figure.

1.
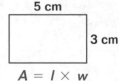
5 cm

3 cm

$A = l \times w$
$A = 5 \text{ cm} \times 3 \text{ cm} = 15 \text{ cm}^2$

2.
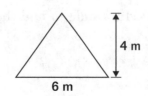
4 m

6 m

3.

2 yd

4.
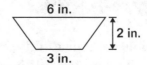
6 in.

2 in.

3 in.

LESSON 19   Properties of Solids

In this lesson you will learn about prisms and pyramids. These solids have faces that are **polygons**. **Prisms** have two congruent bases that are parallel polygons. The sides are all parallelograms.

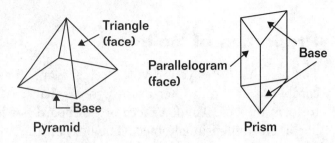

To find the volume of a prism, you multiply the area of the base times the height between the bases. Each corner point is called a vertex.

A pyramid has only one base and the sides are all triangles.

The volume of a pyramid is equal to $\frac{1}{3}$ of the area of the base times the height between the base and the vertex that is not on the base. So to find the volume of a prism or pyramid, you need to remember how to find the area of the polygon that makes up the base.

Here are the general volume formulas:

Volume of a:

prism = area of the base × height or V = Bh

pyramid = $\dfrac{1}{3}$ × area of the base × height or V = $\dfrac{1}{3}$ Bh

Because you are multiplying three units of length together, the units of volume are cubed, like in.^{3} or m^3 or ft^3.

Example

Find the volume of this rectangular prism.

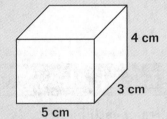

STEP 1 Find the area of the base.
The base is a rectangle and so the area = 3 cm × 5 cm = 15 cm^2.

STEP 2 Find the height
The height is 4 centimeters.

STEP 3 Use the correct formula to find the volume.
The solid is a prism, so Volume = 15 cm^2 × 4 cm = 60 cm^3.

The volume is 60 cm^3.

ON YOUR OWN

Find the volume of this prism that has right triangle bases.

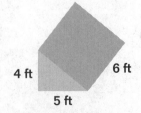

Practice

Building Skills

Find the volume of each solid.

1.

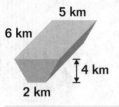

5 km
6 km
4 km
2 km

The base area is (2 km + 5 km) $\times$ 4 km $\times \frac{1}{2} = 14$ km². The height of the prism is 6 km, so 6 km $\times$ 14 km² = 84 km³.

2.

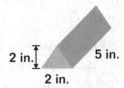

3 mi
2 mi
6 mi

3.

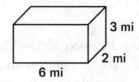

2 in. 5 in.
2 in.

4.

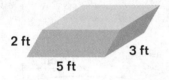

2 ft
3 ft
5 ft

5.

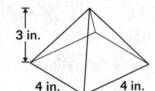

3 in.
4 in.   4 in.

6.

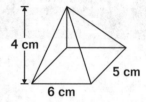

4 cm
5 cm
6 cm

7.

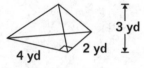

3 yd
2 yd
4 yd

8.

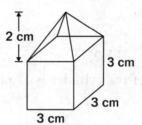

2 cm
3 cm
3 cm
3 cm

9.

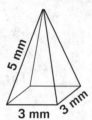

5 mm
3 mm 3 mm

Problem Solving

Solve using properties of solids.

10. You buy your little sister a wading pool. It is a 4-ft by 6-ft rectangular prism. How many cubic feet of water would it take to fill it 1.5 ft deep?

4 ft $\times$ 6 ft $\times$ 1.5 ft = 36 ft³

11. Your square cake pans are all 9 in. by 9 in. by 2 in. high. What will be the volume of the cake if you make three layers using these pans (if all pans are filled to the top)?

12. A box for a granola bar is shaped like a triangular prism. The triangles are 2 in. wide and 1.5 in. high, and the triangular bases are 10 in. apart. What is the volume of the box?

13. The Great Pyramid of Giza is a square pyramid with base sides of about 230 m and a height of about 150 m. Using these measurements, what is its volume?

Surface Area Using Nets: Cylinder

When you peel an orange or a banana, you take a three-dimensional shape and end up with a peel that can be laid out flat. That is the basic idea behind nets. A net is the flattened out peel of a 3-D shape. In this lesson you will look at the nets of cylinders.

Think of the shape of a soda can. What did it look like before it was put together? It had to have a circular top, a circular bottom, and a rectangle that was wrapped around the circles to create the side of the can. The total area would be the area of the two circles plus the area of the rectangle.

You know the formula for the area of a circle. It is $A = \pi \times r^2$. You also know the formula for the area of a rectangle. It is $A = l \times w$. By using these two formulas and the idea of nets, you can find the surface area of any cylinder.

surface area of can

Example

Find the surface area of this cylinder. Use 3.14 for π.

STEP 1 Find the radius and the height.
$r = 4$ cm, $h = 3$ cm

STEP 2 Put them into the formula.
$SA = 2\pi r^2 + 2\pi rh$
$SA = 2 \times (3.14 \times (4 \text{ cm})^2) + (2 \times 3.14 \times 4 \text{ cm}) \times 3 \text{ cm}$
$= 100.48 \text{ cm}^2 + 75.36 \text{ cm}^2 = 175.84 \text{ cm}^2$

The surface area of the cylinder is 175.84 cm^2.

4 cm

3 cm

ON YOUR OWN

What is the surface area of a cylinder with radius 2 in. and height 4 in.? Use 3.14 for π.

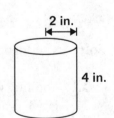

2 in.

4 in.

Practice

Building Skills

Find the surface area. Use 3.14 for π.

1.

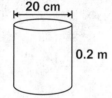

2 ft   5 ft

> If the diameter is 2 ft, then the
> radius is 1 ft. The height is 5 ft, so
> the surface area is $2 \times (\pi \times (1 \text{ ft})^2)$
> $+ (2 \times \pi \times 1 \text{ ft}) \times 5 \text{ ft} = 37.68 \text{ ft}^2$

2.

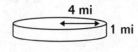

4 mi   1 mi

3.

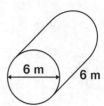

6 m   6 m

4.

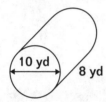

10 yd   8 yd

5.

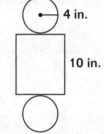

4 in.   10 in.

6.

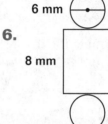

6 mm   8 mm

7.

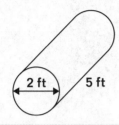

20 cm   0.2 m

8.

4 ft   6.28 ft

9.

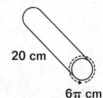

20 cm 6π cm

Problem Solving

Solve. Use the formula to find the surface area of a cylinder. Use 3.14 for π.

10. A juice can is about 6 in. high and 2 in. in diameter. How much metal is needed to make a can with these dimensions?

> $\text{SA} = 2\pi r(r + h)$;
> $\text{SA} = 2 \times 3.14 \times 1(1 + 6) = 43.96 \text{ in.}^2$

11. You are packing up a cylindrical drum to take to a show. It has a diameter of 18 in. and a height of 6 in. How much bubble wrap will you need to cover it?

12. A muffin is almost cylindrical, with a height of 4 cm and a diameter of 10 cm. How much area is there to cover in one well of a muffin pan with butter spray?

13. You and your father are going to wrap your water heater to insulate it and save money. It is 4 ft high and 2 ft in diameter. How much insulation will it take to cover the sides and the top only?

Surface Area Using Nets: Rectangular Prisms

This solid is called a rectangular prism, and as you learned with cylinders, nets can be used to find the surface area. If you take a cardboard box and cut it along the edges, you will get a net made up of six rectangles.

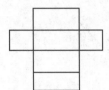

Each of the shapes in the net is a rectangle, and each one is the same as (or congruent to) the rectangle that was opposite it on the solid. To find the surface area of the rectangular prism, you add up all of the rectangle areas. Each rectangle has two of the three dimensions of the solid.

The total formula for the surface area of a rectangular solid is:
$$SA = 2\,(l \times w) + 2\,(l \times h) + 2\,(w \times h)$$
where l, w, and h are the length, width, and height of the solid.

Example

Find the surface area of the box below.

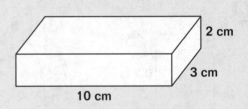

STEP 1 Find the length, width, and height of the solid.
$l = 10$ cm, $w = 3$ cm, and $h = 2$ cm

STEP 2 Use the formula.
$$SA = 2(10 \text{ cm} \times 3 \text{ cm}) + 2(10 \text{ cm} \times 2 \text{ cm}) + 2(3 \text{ cm} \times 2 \text{ cm})$$
$$= 2(30 \text{ cm}^2) + 2(20 \text{ cm}^2) + 2(6 \text{ cm}^2) = 112 \text{ cm}^2$$

The surface area of the box is 112 cm².

ON YOUR OWN

Find the surface area of the box below.

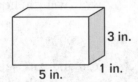

Practice

Building Skills

Find the surface area.

1.

$SA = 2(2 \text{ m} \times 2 \text{ m}) + 2(2 \text{ m} \times 2 \text{ m}) + 2(2 \text{ m} \times 2 \text{ m}) = 24 \text{ m}^2$

2.

3.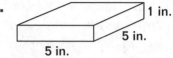

4.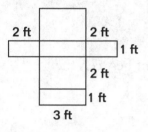

5.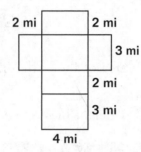

6.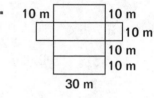

Problem Solving

Use nets to solve these problems.

7. A shipping box with a total area of 350 sq in. has a length of 15 in. and a width of 10 in. How high is the box?

$350 \text{ in.}^2 = 2(15 \text{ in.} \times 10 \text{ in.}) + 2(15 \text{ in.} \times h \text{ in.}) + 2(10 \text{ in.} \times h \text{ in.})$, so $350 \text{ in.}^2 = 300 \text{ in.}^2 + 30 \text{ in.} \times h + 20 \text{ in.} \times h = 300 \text{ in.}^2 + 50 \text{ in.} \times h \text{ in.}$ Finally $50 \text{ in.}^2 = 50 \text{ in.} \times h \text{ in.}$, and so $h = 1$; the height is 1 in.

8. You are painting a toy box for your nephew. The toy box is a rectangular prism that is 2 ft wide by 3 ft long by 2 ft high. How much surface do you need to paint (leave out the bottom)?

9. How many cm^2 of wrap will it take to cover a CD case that is 1 cm high by 10 cm wide by 12 cm long?

10. You have enough paint to cover 400 sq ft. Will it be enough to paint the ceiling and walls of a room that is 10 ft wide by 10 ft long, by 8 ft high (minus 15 ft^2 for a door and window)? Explain.

11. You are asked to cover your textbook. Your textbook is 10 in. long, 8 in. wide, and 1 in. high. What is the surface area of the front, the spine, and the back cover?

12. You are wrapping a present in a box that is 2 ft by 1 ft by 1 ft. How much paper would it take to cover the box if you do not overlap any of it?

LESSON 22   Volume of a Cylinder

You want to know how much a can of soup or vegetables holds. But if the base is not a rectangle or triangle, how can you find how much the can holds?

When you started this unit, you learned about the volumes of prisms and pyramids. Volumes of those solids depended on the areas of the bases and their heights. Cylinders use the same idea, but the bases are both circles. Once again, because these are circles, you need to use the number π (called pi and equal to about 3.14).

$A = \pi \times r^2$

$C = 2 \times \pi \times r$

The volume of a cylinder is equal to the area of the circle times the height between the circular bases.

The formula is: Volume $= \pi \times$ radius$^2 \times$ height or $V = \pi \times r^2 \times h$

Example

What is the volume of the cylinder below? Use 3.14 for π.

STEP 1 Find the radius and height of the cylinder.
The radius is half the diameter $r = 2$ ft, the height is 5 ft.

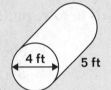

STEP 2 Use the formula.
$V = 3.14 \times (2 \text{ ft})^2 \times 5 \text{ ft} = 3.14 \times 4 \text{ ft}^2 \times 5 \text{ ft} = 62.8 \text{ ft}^3$

The volume of the cylinder is 62.8 ft^3.

ON YOUR OWN

Find the volume of the cylinder below.

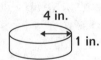

Practice

Radius is half the diameter.

Building Skills

Find the volume. Use 3.14 for π.

1.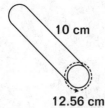

10 cm

12.56 cm

> The radius is 2 cm, and the height is 10 cm. The volume is $\pi \times (2 \text{ cm})^2 \times 10 \text{ cm} = 125.6 \text{ cm}^3$.

2.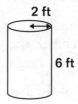

2 ft

6 ft

3.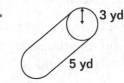

3 yd

5 yd

4.

10 cm

12 cm

5.

5 cm

31.4 cm

6.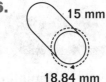

15 mm

18.84 mm

Problem Solving

Use volume to solve these problems. Use 3.14 for π.

7. A can of soup measures 10 cm high by 6 cm in diameter. What is the volume of soup it contains?

> $r = 3$ cm, and $h = 10$ cm, $V = 3.14 \times (3 \text{ cm})^2 \times 10 \text{ cm} = 282.6 \text{ cm}^3$

8. A bucket of popcorn at the movies is a cylinder with a radius of 6 in. and a height of 10 in. What volume of popcorn can it hold?

9. A subway tunnel is a cylinder with a radius of 4 m and a length between the ends of 1,000 m. What is the volume of dirt workers need to remove to make this tunnel?

10. A can of tennis balls has a 3-in. diameter and is 10 in. high? What is the volume of space inside?

11. Your trash can is 15 in. high and has a diameter of 12 in. What is the volume of trash that you can put inside the trash can?

12. You measure a can that holds 16 oz of juice. It is 14 cm tall and has a diameter of 6 cm. How much space is needed to hold 16 oz?

Volume of a Cone

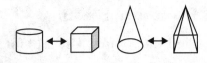

Just as a cylinder is like a prism, a cone is similar to a pyramid. The difference in the formula for the volume of a cylinder and a prism is in their bases. The base of a prism is a polygon. The base of a cylinder is a circle. A cone is just a pyramid with a circle for a base.

Because a cone is a pyramid with a circle base, the formulas for finding the volume of a cone and a pyramid are almost the same. Remember, the general formula for the volume of a pyramid is $V = \frac{1}{3} \times$ area of the base $\times$ height.

This formula is the same for cones, but the area of the base is a circle, and so it equals π times the radius squared. By changing the pyramid formula slightly, you will have the formula for cones. Volume of a cone $= \frac{1}{3} \times \pi \times r^2 \times h$

The height is always the distance between the circle and the top point of the cone, no matter how the cone is turned.

Example

Find the volume of the cone. Use 3.14 for π.

STEP 1 Find the radius and the height.
$r = 2$ in. and $h = 6$ in.

2 in. ⟂

6 in.

STEP 2 Use the formula.
Volume of a cone $= \frac{1}{3} \times 3.14 \times r^2 \times h = \frac{1}{3} \times 3.14 \times (2 \text{ in.})^2 \times 6$ in.
$= \frac{1}{3} \times 3.14 \times 4 \text{ in.}^2 \times 6 \text{ in.} = \frac{1}{3} \times 3.14 \times 24 \text{ in.}^3$
$= 25.12$ in.^{3}

The volume of the cone is 25.12 in.^{3}

ON YOUR OWN

What is the volume of this cone?

3 cm

5 cm

Practice

Building Skills

Find the volume. Use 3.14 for π.

1.

3 km

6.28 km

> The circumference is 6.28 km so the radius is 1 km, and the height is 3 km. The volume is $\frac{1}{3} \times 3.14 \times (1 \text{ km})^2 \times 3 \text{ km} = 3.14 \text{ km}^3$.

2.

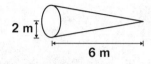

2 m

6 m

3.

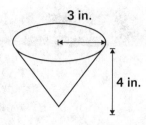

3 in.

4 in.

4.

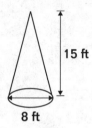

15 ft

8 ft

5.

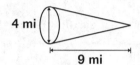

4 mi

9 mi

6.

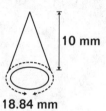

10 mm

18.84 mm

Problem Solving

Solve. Use 3.14 for π.

7. How many cubic centimeters of ice cream fit in a cone with a diameter of 4 cm, and a height of 12 cm.

> $r = 2$ cm, $h = 12$ cm so $V = \frac{1}{3} \times 3.14$ $(2 \text{ cm})^2 \times 12 \text{ cm} = 50.24 \text{ cm}^3$

8. An insect called a sand lion digs holes that are cone-shaped in the sand. How much sand did the sand lion need to clear out to make a hole that is 20 mm deep and has a radius of 12 mm?

9. What is the volume of a traffic cone that is 3 ft high and has a diameter of 1 ft?

10. What is the volume of a funnel that has a 4 in. diameter, and is 3 in. high?

11. At the costume party, Sandra wore a pointed hat. She needed something to keep her wallet in, so she turned over her hat and used the hat as a purse. If the circumference of the hat is about 12.56 in., and it is 24 in. high, what is the volume of the hat?

12. A cone-shaped pile of sand is 5 ft high, and has a diameter of 6 ft. How many cubic feet of sand are in this pile?

TEST–TAKING STRATEGY

Write an Equation

Writing an equation using a formula can help you answer test questions about volume.

Example

The Aquadom Aquarium in Berlin, Germany is the largest cylinder aquarium in the world. It has a radius of 18 ft and a height of 52 ft. Estimate the volume of the aquarium. Use 3.14 for π.

STEP 1 Write the formula for finding the volume of a cylinder.
Remember: A formula is an equation that shows a relationship between two or more amounts.

Volume of a cylinder = area of the base times the height
$V = Bh$
$V = \pi r^2 h$ — Think: The base of a cylinder is a circle. The formula for finding the area of a circle is $A = \pi r^2$.

STEP 2 Use the formula to estimate the volume of the aquarium. Round each number to the greatest place.
$V = \pi r^2 h$
$V = 3.14 \times 18^2 \times 52$ rounds to
$V \approx 3 \times 20^2 \times 50$
$V \approx 3 \times 400 \times 50$
$V \approx 60{,}000$

The volume of the aquarium is about 60,000 ft³.

TRY IT OUT

A wastebasket is the shape of a cylinder. It has a radius of 11 cm and a height of 32 cm. Round to the greatest place to estimate the volume of the wastebasket.

Circle the correct answer.

A. about 300 cm³   **B.** about 900 cm³   **C.** about 3,000 cm³   **D.** about 9,000 cm³

Option D is correct. To estimate the volume of the wastebasket, you multiply $3 \times 10^2 \times 30$ which equals 9,000 cm³.

Find the volume.

1. rectangular solid

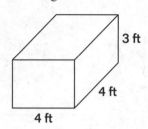

3 ft
4 ft
4 ft

2. triangular prism

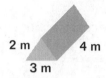

2 m   4 m
3 m

3. square pyramid

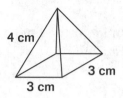

4 cm
3 cm
3 cm

4. rectangular pyramid

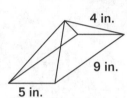

4 in.
9 in.
5 in.

5. cylinder

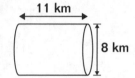

11 km
8 km

6. cone

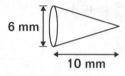

6 mm
10 mm

Find the surface area.

7. rectangular prism

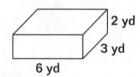

2 yd
3 yd
6 yd

8. net

3 cm   3 cm
        4 cm
        3 cm
        4 cm
5 cm

9. net of a cylinder

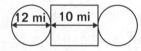

12 mi   10 mi

10. cylinder

3 m
4 m

Solve using volume.

11. How much room is there in a locker that is 6 in. wide 10 in. deep and 5 ft high?

12. A juice can has a radius of 3 cm and a height of 15 cm. What is its volume?

Post Test

Take this Post Test after you have completed this book. The Post Test will help you determine how far you have progressed in building your math skills.

Determine if the lines are parallel, perpendicular, or intersecting but not perpendicular.

1. 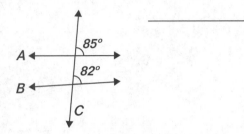 _____

2. 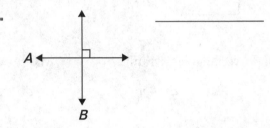 _____

Identify each angle as acute, right, obtuse, or straight.

3.  _____

4. 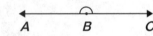 _____

Find the supplement for each angle.

5. 125° _____

6. 90° _____

Use this diagram for problems 7 and 8.

7. Identify any radii of the circle A. _____

8. If *BA* measures 20 yards, find the diameter of circle A.

Find the area of each figure.

9. 8 in. 20 in. □

10. 10 mi 2.5 mi △

Use the similar figures in this diagram to answer questions 11 and 12.

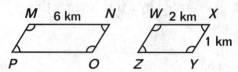

11. How long is side *MP*?

12. What angle corresponds to ∠*O*?

Find the coordinates of each point after the given transformation.

13. Where is the image of point $(-3, -7)$ after a $(2, 6)$ slide?

14. Where is the image of point $(3, -4)$ after a flip over the *x*-axis?

15. Where is the image of point $(5, 8)$ after a $90°$ clockwise rotation

16. Where is the image of point $(10, -4)$ after a dilation with its center at $(0, 0)$ and a scale factor of 3?

Find the volume of each figure. Turn to page 77 for a list of formulas.

17.

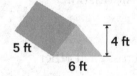

5 ft   4 ft

6 ft

18.

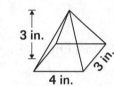

3 in.

4 in.   3 in.

Find each surface area. Turn to page 78 for a list of formulas.

19.

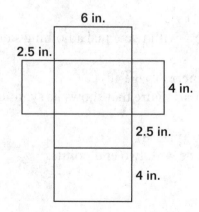

6 in.

2.5 in.

4 in.

2.5 in.

4 in.

20.

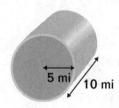

5 mi   10 mi

Glossary

acute angle (page 12)
an angle whose measure is less than 90°

acute triangle (page 20)
a triangle in which all angles are acute angles

angle (page 12)
when two lines intersect at a point

area (page 32)
the measure of the space inside a flat figure;
area of a parallelogram $= l \times w$,
the area of a triangle $= \frac{1}{2}bh$

base (page 59)
any side in a parallelogram or triangle; the
bottom of a three-dimensional shape

center point (page 54)
the point from which all distances are measured
when a figure is dilated

chord (page 24)
a line segment whose endpoints lie on the circle

circle (page 24)
a closed set of infinite points on a line

circumference (page 26)
the distance around the edge of a circle

complementary angles (page 14)
two angles whose sum is 90°

cone (page 68)
a three-dimensional figure that has a circular
base, a vertex, and a curved surface

congruent figures (page 38)
figures that have the same shape and size

coordinate plane (page 47)
a horizontal number line (the x-axis) crossed
with a vertical number line (the y-axis)

corresponding angles (page 14)
two equal angles formed by a line intersecting
two parallel lines

cylinder (page 62)
a three-dimensional figure with two congruent
circular bases that are parallel to each other

diameter (page 24)
a chord that goes through the center of the circle

dilation (page 54)
to expand or reduce a figure in size while
keeping the same shape

equilateral triangle (page 20)
a triangle in which all sides are congruent
lengths

face (page 60)
a polygon that forms one of the surfaces of a
three-dimensional figure

image (page 48)
new figure after a transformation

intersect (page 10)
when lines or planes cross each other

isosceles triangle (page 20)
a triangle in which two sides are congruent
lengths

kite (page 22)
a quadrilateral with two equal adjoining sides

line of symmetry (page 40)
the line across a figure that shows its symmetry

line segment (page 8)
a part of a line with two end points

line (page 8)
a straight path that extends without end in opposite directions

net (page 62)
a two-dimensional pattern that can be folded to form a three-dimensional figure

obtuse angle (page 12)
an angle whose measure is greater than 90°

obtuse triangle (page 20)
a triangle with an obtuse angle

origin (page 48)
the point where the *x*-axis and *y*-axis cross

parallel lines (page 10)
lines in the same plane that never intersect

parallelogram (page 22)
a quadrilateral with two pairs of parallel sides

perpendicular lines (page 10)
lines that intersect to form right angles

pi (π) (page 26)
the ratio of the circumference of a circle to its diameter; equal to approximately 3.14

plane (page 8)
a flat surface that goes on forever

point of rotation (page 52)
another term for the turn center

point (page 8)
an exact location

polygon (page 22)
a flat, closed figure with at least three sides

prism (page 60)
a three-dimensional figure that has two congruent bases that are parallel polygons

protractor (page 12)
an instrument used to measure angles

pyramid (page 60)
a three-dimensional figure in which one face, the base, is a polygon, and the other faces are triangles that meet at a common point, call the vertex

Pythagorean theorem (page 42)
a formula used to find lengths of sides in a right triangle; $a^2 + b^2 = c^2$

quadrilateral (page 22)
a polygon with four sides, four angles, and four vertices

radius (page 24)
the distance from the center of the circle to the edge

ray (page 8)
has one endpoint and goes without stopping in one direction only

rectangle (page 22)
a quadrilateral with four right angles

reflection (page 50)
flipping a figure over a given line

rhombus (page 22)
a quadrilateral with four equal, parallel sides

right angle (page 12)
an angle whose measure is 90°

right triangle (page 20)
a triangle with a right angle

Glossary

rotation (page 52)
a transformation in which a figure is turned about a point a certain number of degrees

scale factor (page 54)
the ratio of a dilated image to the original figure

scalene triangle (page 20)
a triangle in which all the sides are different lengths

similar figures (page 38)
figures that have the same proportions

slide coordinates (page 48)
coordinates that show the direction and the distance of a slide

solid (page 59)
another term for a three-dimensional shape

square (page 22)
a quadrilateral with four equal sides and four right angles

straight angle (page 12)
an angle whose measure is 180°

supplementary angles (page 14)
two angles whose sum is 180°

surface area (page 62)
the sum of the areas of all the faces and bases of a prism, cylinder, pyramid, or cone; for a sphere it is four times the area of a great circle

symmetry (page 40)
a figure can be folded or moved so that two parts of the figure match

three-dimensional shape (page 59)
a shape that has height, as well as length and width, also called a three-dimensional shape

transformation (page 46)
a change in the position, size, or shape of a geometric figure

translation (page 48)
sliding a figure to a new location

trapezoid (page 22)
a quadrilateral with only one pair of parallel sides

triangle (page 22)
a polygon with 3 sides, 3 angles, and 3 vertices

turn center (page 52)
point around which a figure is rotated

vertex (page 12)
the point where lines come together to form an angle; a corner point

vertical angles (page 14)
opposite angles formed by intersecting lines

Math Toolkit

Important Formulas and Common Geometric Shapes

Perimeter	
Square	$P = 4s$
Rectangle	$P = 2l + 2w$
Circumference of a circle	$C = \pi d$ or $C = 2\pi r$
Area	
Square	$A = s^2$
Rectangle	$A = lw$
Parallelogram	$A = bh$
Triangle	$A = \frac{1}{2}bh$
Circle	$A = \pi r^2$
Volume	
Cube	$V = s^3$
Rectangular solid	$V = lwh$
Cylinder	$V = \pi r^2 h$
Pythagorean theorem	$a^2 + b^2 = c^2$
Pyramid	$V = \frac{1}{3}Bh$
Rectangular Prism	$V = lwh$
Cone	$V = \frac{1}{3}\pi r^2 h$

Square

$P = 4s$

$A = s^2$

Triangle

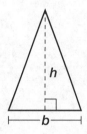

$A = \frac{1}{2}bh$

Rhombus

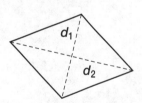

$A = \frac{1}{2}d_1 d_2$

Rectangle

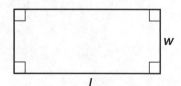

$P = 2l + 2w$

$A = lw$

Trapezoid

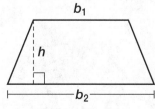

$A = \frac{1}{2}h(b_1 + b_2)$

Parallelogram

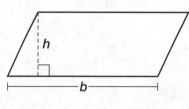

$A = bh$

Math Toolkit

Formulas for Surface Area

The surface area of a space figure is the sum if all the faces of the figure. Following are the formulas for finding the surface area of several figures.

Cube

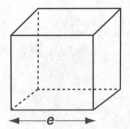

$$SA = 6e^2$$

where e = the length of an edge.

Prism

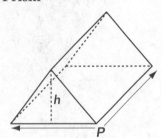

$$SA = 2B + Ph$$

where B = the area of the base, P = the perimeter of the base, and h = the height of the prism.

Cylinder

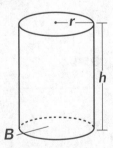

$$SA = 2\pi r^2 + 2\pi rh$$

where r = the radius of the circle and h = the height of the cylinder.

Cone

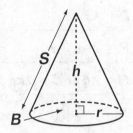

$$SA = \pi r^2 + \pi rs$$

where r = the radius of the circle and s = the slant height.

Pyramid

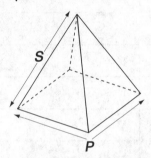

$$SA = B + \frac{1}{2}Ps$$

where B = the area of the base, P = the perimeter of the base, and s = the slant height of the lateral faces.

Sphere

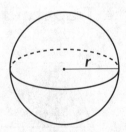

$$SA = 4\pi r^2$$

where r = the radius of the sphere.